Making the Most of Your Greenhouse

Gardening Concorde Books

BASIC GARDENING
CACTI AND OTHER SUCCULENT PLANTS
CLIMBERS AND WALL PLANTS
FLOWER ARRANGING
FRUIT GROWING MONTH BY MONTH
GARDEN PESTS AND DISEASES
GARDENING FOR BEGINNERS
GROUND COVER PLANTS
GROWING FROM CUTTINGS
GROWING INDOOR PLANTS
GROWING VEGETABLES AND HERBS
HOUSE PLANTS
HOW TO GROW AND USE HERBS
MAKING AND PLANNING A SMALL GARDEN
MAKING THE MOST OF YOUR GREENHOUSE
PRACTICAL PRUNING
SHRUBS AND DECORATIVE EVERGREENS
SIMPLE FRUIT GROWING
SIMPLE GARDEN CONSTRUCTION
SIMPLE GREENHOUSE GARDENING
SIMPLE PLANT PROPAGATION
SIMPLE TOMATO GROWING
SIMPLE VEGETABLE GROWING
SUCCESSFUL BONSAI GROWING
TREES FOR GARDENS
VEGETABLE GROWING MONTH BY MONTH
WINDOW BOXES, TUBS AND PATIOS

Making the Most of Your Greenhouse

Ian Walls

Ward Lock Limited · London

© Ward Lock Limited 1975

Paperback ISBN 0 7063 1949 4

First published in Great Britain 1975
by Ward Lock Limited,
47 Marylebone Lane, London. W1M 6AX, a Pentos Company
Reprinted 1977, 1981

Text filmset by Type Practitioners Ltd
Printed in England by
Fakenham Press Limited, Fakenham, Norfolk.

Contents

Preface

Today more and more keen gardeners are buying greenhouses. Indeed, a greenhouse is about as essential in a modern garden as a spade. The simile is very apt: a greenhouse is simply a tool — a device for overcoming the vagaries and limitations of an uncertain climate and enabling the keen gardener to raise and grow crops and plants which would fail altogether out of doors or else be very slow to develop.

Like any other tool, a greenhouse is only as good as the use you make of it, and the ingenuity you exercise in finding ways of using it more and more effectively. Run on old-fashioned lines, a greenhouse is a time-consuming hobby, where you spend most of your life doing endless chores — and often losing plants because you did not have time to carry out one vital chore at one vital moment. Run on modern lines, with the aid of all the modern devices now available, a greenhouse is an almost completely automatic, self-maintaining system where all you have to do is enjoy the plants.

The purpose of this short book is to show you ways of getting the best out of your greenhouse by making the most of the ingenious modern devices available to help you run it. The whole range of equipment is discussed, briefly, and in plain language so that you can understand exactly what it is all about. A full understanding of this will in turn enable you to grow bigger and better crops over a longer period of the year — something which is very important in these days of endlessly spiralling prices of fruits, vegetables and pot plants.

1 First Principles

A greenhouse, whatever its size or shape, whatever it is made from, and whatever it looks like, has only one reason for existing, and that is to create a largely articifical, wholly controllable and totally reliable climate in which you can raise and grow plants which you could not rely upon thriving in the vagaries of the harsher climate outside. In its most basic form a greenhouse could be regarded simply as a glass box designed to trap the energy from sunlight — and that energy includes both light and heat. Plants need this energy to grow. Curiously enough, the light is more important than the heat — so far as growing goes. Heat only becomes important when we try to grow plants that cannot endure low temperatures such as those experienced at high latitudes.

Although experts still do not agree on what shape the ideal greenhouse should be, there is one thing they all agree on. That is that whatever sort of greenhouse you buy, the one with the largest panes and the smallest astragals (struts) will be the most efficient sun energy trap.

Having gone to the trouble of making sure that you have an efficient sun energy trap, you obviously do not want to waste its potential by placing it in the shade of tall trees, buildings or hedges. In this context it is worth remembering that, because the sun is lower in the sky in winter than in summer, the shadows it casts are longer. Make allowance for this if you are working out where to put your greenhouse in mid-summer. Any shadows will be at least four times longer in winter — and that is when your greenhouse needs its sun energy. On the other hand, buildings, hedges and trees can be useful: they can give valuable shelter from cold winds that could cool the greenhouse unduly.

While heat is important in the greenhouse in winter, it is worth remembering that a greenhouse is such an efficient sun energy trap that it can actually overheat in summer — getting far too hot either for your own comfort or for the plants. This is something that was not realised until relatively recently and is still not appreciated by many greenhouse owners. Indeed, probably more plants are lost through overheating in summer than through under-heating in winter. When considering automation for the greenhouse, ventilation and cooling controls are just as vital as heaters and heating controls.

Indeed, so efficient is the greenhouse at converting the energy from sunlight into heat that scientists all over the world are busy exploring the possibilities of heating homes with energy from sunlight by means of structures very similar to greenhouses. Ironically, they have not yet worked out a way of heating your greenhouse in winter with the stored surplus energy it accumulates in summer. But that may not be too far in the future.

Greenhouses come in all sorts of different shapes and sizes and face all sorts of directions, according to how they happen to fit into a garden. Those which catch the most sun, especially in winter, are those which have their long sides facing south, or almost south. Some are specially designed to catch relatively more sun in winter than in summer — all a matter of the angle of the glass on the sides. Lean-to greenhouses against the wall of a house or garage catch almost too much sun in summer. They can get so intensely hot in summer that it is difficult to keep them cool even with all the ventilators or doors open, which means that you will probably have to put up some form of shading to shut out some of the sun, especially for many pot plants.

When it comes to heating it, then a good supply of electricity or, in these days, natural gas is also desirable. But do be sure that it has been properly installed by a tradesman and not by a do-it-yourself enthusiast who does not really know what he is doing — and this could mean you! If you are installing heating bear in mind that it is a greenhouse you are heating and try to trap as much of costly generated heat as possible by sealing up air leaks or badly fitting doors and vents.

A convenient water supply is also essential, since few things are more of a bore than running about with watering cans. Water supply pipes to greenhouses are best laid deeply in the ground below the level of potential frost damage, or as a compromise a hose pipe from a stand pipe at the garage would also do well.

Something else worth thinking about, if you have not already done so, is getting rid of all the rain water shed by the greenhouse roof. Whether your greenhouse has a gutter or not, the rain must go somewhere and this should preferably not be where it seeps into the greenhouse foundations, making everything soaking wet and causing unsightly moss and algae to grow. Besides, with perpetual threats of water shortages and rationing, the rain water off a greenhouse roof can keep a water butt well supplied in most seasons. Most manufacturers supply plastic guttering as an optional extra.

CARE AND MAINTENANCE OF GREENHOUSES

Greenhouses are, in many ways, like cars. They will continue to operate but quickly deteriorate, with gradual lowering of efficiency, if not given a regular service. Fortunately greenhouses seldom require servicing as regularly as cars — about once a year on average.

Pressure treated wood greenhouses should merely be washed down inside and out and all moss and algae removed with a brush and a bucket of warm detergent, followed by a jet of water from a hose. When there are overlaps in the glass, this is a convenient spot for the build up of algae and a piece of thin metal is useful to remove this. Moss can frequently collect on the greenhouse astragals or glazing bars on the outside of the greenhouse, especially on the less sunny side, and this should be brushed off with a stiff brush.

Whether you paint a wooden greenhouse or not may be a matter of necessity or of choice. Pressure treated dry glazed greenhouses can last for 15-20 years or more without any painting, but certainly look a bit dowdy. When wood is untreated it **must** be painted at least every 3 or 4 years, or more frequently if appearance is important. However, while a pressure treated dry glazed greenhouse can be left unpainted for years, there are good reasons for painting it. A well painted greenhouse admits more light due to the reflective qualities of white paint. Paints for greenhouses are now nearly all of the organic oil and synthetic resin type. White lead paint is now more or less out of use. Lead is both expensive and poisonous.

It should seldom be necessary to paint an alloy greenhouse. Steel greenhouses, even though galvanised, will certainly require painting eventually. Aluminium paint is useful here, provided the metal is clean and not rusty before it is applied. If it is rusty, clean off loose rust with a wire brush and stabilize the rusting process with a proprietary product designed for just that purpose.

Greenhouse glazing systems must be kept in good order, not only for your own safety and the avoidance of damage by high winds, but also to prevent drips. Glazing strip materials are very useful here when the glazing system deteriorates. This applies especially to putty glazing systems when the putty goes hard and cracks. Glazing strips are also useful for the odd cracks in the glass which develop, especially when the pane sizes are large, as glass is becoming a very expensive commodity.

The outside of glass can require cleaning, especially in industrial areas. A strong detergent will remove most of the grime from glass and let in maximum light.

Base walls of greenhouses (if any) will benefit from a coating of emulsion or weather-proof paint, both inside and out.

2 Heating Your Greenhouse

It is because greenhouses are efficient sun traps and absorb heat from the sun readily, that they also lose heat almost as quickly when the sun stops shining. When the outside temperature drops down below frost level, the temperature of the air inside your greenhouse, if unheated, will be almost as cold as it is out of doors. Try using a couple of maximum/minimum thermometers (you can always borrow them) — one inside the greenhouse and one out of doors, and you will see how little difference there is between the two. The more glass there is in your greenhouse the nearer the temperatures inside and outside will be to each other. The old fashioned greenhouse with a heavy brick base wall and constructed of thick wooden bars and small panes of glass will keep a lot warmer than an all-glass alloy structure. But when the sun shines, the all-glass structure will be a lot quicker to warm up.

Think a little about this and you will come to the obvious conclusion that it will cost a lot more to heat a modern alloy greenhouse than it will an old-fashioned wooden one, but once the warm days come in spring the alloy greenhouse will be a brighter and better place to grow your plants.

Think still more about it and it becomes clear also that how much you are prepared to spend on heating your greenhouse will largely determine what range of plants one can grow. Or to put it another way, you may decide that you only want to grow plants between spring and autumn, when not much articifical heat will be required in the greenhouse and you can rely mainly on warmth from the sun.

12

A maximum/minimum thermometer positioned near rod thermostats to give as accurate a reading as possible

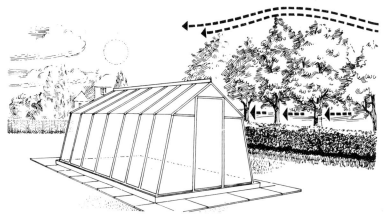

Diagram of a greenhouse showing the use of trees and hedges to break the force of wind

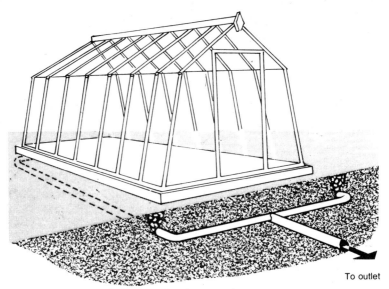

To outlet

Diagram showing the drainage system in a greenhouse

There are some plants, just like people, which are able to stand up to the cold whereas others do not. If you want to grow a few tomatoes, which are warm blooded plants and come from near the Equator, then you will simply have to wait until the weather is warm enough and there is little risk of frost, before growing them in a completely cold greenhouse.

So before even beginning to think in terms of what kind or size of heater to buy, it is worth taking the time to examine this whole business of what level of heat different plants require, not only if they are to simply survive, but grow well and produce flowers and fruit or whatever it is you are growing them for.

What is more important perhaps, in these days of high fuel costs, is to avoid using too much heat when a little less will do. Even a degree or two higher temperature over the course of a few weeks can result in a big difference to your electricity, oil, coal or gas bills. It is therefore worth taking a close look at the different temperature levels, since they determine not only what you can grow but also what it will cost you to heat your greenhouse.

There are four general heat levels to consider.

Stove Conditions (S)

As the name implies, this means keeping a greenhouse very hot all the time, at the sort of temperature you will find in the Palm House at Kew or any other botanical garden housing collections of tropical plants. Only the enthusiastic grower of tender orchids without heed of the expense involved would be prepared to heat to this level. One way of achieving very warm conditions at relatively low cost would be to install the domestic central heating boiler in the greenhouse. In this way the 'waste' heat from the boiler is given off all the time the boiler is in operation, which is pretty well continuously. One obvious problem here is where the domestic boiler is used in hot summer weather for domestic hot water, this being the sort of situation which could perhaps be overcome by having an immersion heater for the hot water which is only used during the summer period.

Warm or Hot Conditions (H)

Here one is involved in a temperature of not less than about 13°C winter and summer. It is a temperature range which allows most things to be grown well throughout the year. While expensive to maintain such a temperature right through the winter, especially in the north, it is reasonable to expect such temperatures from early spring onwards at not too exhorbitant a cost.

Cool Conditions (FP)

When the greenhouse is to be kept completely frost free (not less than 7°C this is classed as 'cool'. It is the level to which a great many of us are encouraged in view of high fuel costs. Do remember though that after about February or March, according to where you live of course, it can be quite easy to hold about 13°C in a greenhouse heated to frost free level. Localised heat for a separately controlled and heated propagating case can work wonders.

Cold Conditions (C)

Here no heat at all is given and one is completely at the mercy of the weather. Yet a lot can be done in a completely cold greenhouse. A heated propagating case really comes into its own here, failing which a light window in the home can with permission be used for the early heat demanding activities, moving on to the greenhouse as the weather improves.

Guide to Heat Level Likely to be Required

At the end of Chapter 13 I have given a table of plants and their appropriate heat categories. The value of considering this lies in deciding precisely what level of heat is likely to be needed, if any at all, before going to all the bother and expense of buying any kind of heating appliance. Or for that matter arrive at a garden centre to buy your heater without really knowing what size of heater you are looking for. Also remember that the estimate of running costs given in a catalogue of heating equipment often presumes ideal conditions — which seldom exist!

Finding out about Heater Sizes

Forget for the moment any consideration of what type of heating system you are thinking about. Your purpose is simply to find out what size of heating unit is required — whether it is powered by electricity, paraffin, waste oil, gas or coal — or even peat! If you remember what was said in Ch. 1 about glass being efficient in letting sunlight through, remember that it also lets heat out pretty quickly. The other materials your greenhouse is likely to be made of such as wood, alloy, steel, brick or asbestos, also let heat pass through. To find out the 'heat loss' as it is called, you must find out how much or what area of each of the materials is involved.

Look up the manufacturer's specification of your greenhouse or do a little sketch of it on a piece of paper, and even if you have to go out with a tape measure make sure that you have pretty exact measurements of the total surface area of your greenhouse.

Ignore all the little bits of alloy or wood which hold in the glass and concentrate on the total surface area of glass or other material in the case of a brick, asbestos or wooden base walls.

	STOVE CONDITIONS 18°C	Some orchids, palms etc
	WARM CONDITIONS 13°C	Pot plants Early tomatoes Early seed sowing Root cuttings
	COOL CONDITIONS Frost free not less than 17°C	Over wintering many pot plants Dahlias Chrysanthemums Later sowings and plantings of all crops
	COLD CONDITIONS No heat	Almost hardy fruit Later start than above but earlier finish Over wintering doubtful

The different heat levels at which a variety of plants can be grown

The greenhouse shown here is an all glass 3m x 2.4m green-house. Details are as follows:

Sides — 2 sides each
    1.8m x 3m = 2 x 5.4m   = 10.8m^2

Ends — (ignoring the door)
    2 ends 2.4m x 1.8m = 2 x 4.3m   = 8.6m^2

Roof — 2 sides of roof each
    1.3m x 3m = 2 x 3.9m   = 7.8m^2

Gables — 2 gables each 0.6m x 2.4m   = 1.4m^2

Total area of glass = 28.6m^2

The heat loss (or μ values) of glasshouse materials are as follows — this being a figure which allows one third for inadvertent losses through doors, glass overlaps, vents, etc. It shows the number of watts (W) lost per m^2 per hour.

Glass (with glazing bars)	7.94
Brickwork (4½in) — single wall	3.63
Brickwork (9in) — double wall	2.66
Brickwork (11in) — wall of dwelling house, i.e. lean to	1.70
(although in practice heat can come from this, especially backing on a well heated room).	
Concrete (4in)	4.25
Concrete (6in)	3.46
Wood (1in)	2.83
Asbestos; Polythene (all grades)	7.94

If one now applies some calculations to the above, we come up with the following sum:

28.6m^2 @ 7.94 W/m^2 (glass) = 227 W/m^2/h for the 3m x 2.4m all glass greenhouse.

To translate this into still simpler terms, the figure is the heat loss from the greenhouse to the outside air for each °C difference in temperature. That is if it is 10°C in the greenhouse and 9°C out of doors. That is called a one degree lift. For each degree difference the rate of heat loss increases. If it were 10°C in the greenhouse and 0°C out of doors, the temperature difference would be 10°C — a 10° lift. And if the greenhouse must be kept at 10°C then 10 times 227=2,270 watts of heat will be required to put into the greenhouse to retain 10°C.

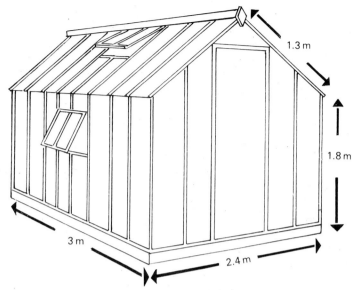

Diagram showing how to calculate heat loss in a greenhouse

There are obviously many different temperatures involved, according not only to how hot you wish to keep your greenhouse, but how cold or windy it can get out of doors. Weather varies all the time and some regions are a lot colder than others. Some areas are not only colder but more exposed, and so on, and all this affects the amount of heat you need. You may only want to use your greenhouse in spring and ignore the winter period entirely.

All one can do is plan for a reasonable degree of warmth despite fairly cold conditions out of doors during the period you want to use the greenhouse and add a little extra for safety as weather out of doors can be unpredictable.

Short cuts to avoid calculations are always attractive and a quick way of working out the *approximate* heat loss for your greenhouse is this:

$$
\left.\begin{array}{l}\text{Square}\\\text{foot}\\\text{floor}\\\text{area}\end{array}\right\} \times \left\{\begin{array}{l}\text{69 for a 11°C 'lift'}\\[6pt]\text{105 for a 16°C 'lift'}\\[6pt]\text{138 for a 22°C 'lift'}\end{array}\right.
$$

Whatever the heat requirement of your greenhouse for a specific temperature range, this is the heat requirement of any type of heating system and only experience will show whether exposure, district, leakiness of structure or other factors result in still bigger heat loss. The tables at the end of the chapter can also be used for quick calculations.

DOUBLE GLAZING
Various types of 'double glazing' can help to reduce the amount of heat your greenhouse loses, which these days is very important. In the home double glazing usually involves double sheets of glass, hermetically sealed, which could be done in your greenhouse but would be frightfully expensive and make the greenhouse far too costly to buy in the first case.

The very simplest yet effective way of double glazing is to line the greenhouse *inside* with thin grade polythene. This will not only reduce heat loss but stop draughts, which is worth while, especially in winter or early spring. Lining with polythene does make the atmosphere of the greenhouse more muggy however and you could find a lot more fungal diseases about. It is easy to tack the polythene on to a wooden greenhouse with drawing pins or a staple gun, but with a metal house wooden straps may need to be rigged up.

Do not cover the vents or fans with the polythene as ventilation is still more important to reduce humidity at times.

If you use plastic sheeting for double glazing your greenhouse you will immediately notice an increase in the amount of condensation forming on the surface. You can spray the plastic sheeting with a modern proprietary chemical to reduce this condensation.

A GUIDE TO ELECTRIC HEATERS AND HEAT REQUIREMENTS GENERALLY
The following guide lines indicate the minimum size of heater for a range of greenhouses under average conditions. The heater will provide a greenhouse temperature of 6°C against an outside temperature of −30°C (9° lift).

GREENHOUSE HEAT REQUIREMENTS

1. Span roof greenhouses — 60 cm brick wall, 2.28 m ridge, 1.3 m eaves

2 x 1.2 m	1 kW	4.2 x 2.4 m	2.75 kW
2 x 2 m	1.25 kW	4.8 x 3 m	3.5 kW
2.4 x 2 m	1.5 kW	5.4 x 3.6 m	4.25 kW
3 x 2 m	1.75 kW	6 x 3.6 m	4.5 kW
3.6 x 2.4 m	2.5 kW		

2. Span roof greenhouses — glass to ground, 2.2 m ridge, 1.3 m eaves

2 x 1.2 m	1.25 kW	4.2 x 2.4 m	3.25 kW
2 x 2 m	1.4 kW	4.8 x 3 m	3.8 kW
2.4 x 2 m	1.5 kW	5.4 x 3.6 m	4.6 kW
3 x 2 m	2.0 kW	6 x 3.6 m	5.5 kW
3.6 x 2.4 m	2.75 kW		

3. Lean-to greenhouses, 60 cm brick or wood base, 2.7 m ridge, 1.3 m eaves

2 x 1.2 m	.75 kW	4.2 x 2.4 m	2.8 kW
2 x 2 m	1.0 kW	4.8 x 3 m	3.3 kW
2.4 x 2 m	1.3 kW	5.4 x 3.6 m	4.0 kW
3 x 2 m	1.5 kW		
3.6 x 2.4 m	2.3 kW		

4. Lean-to greenhouses, glass to ground, 2.7 m ridge, 1.3 m eaves

2 x 1.2 m	1.0 kW	3.6 x 2.4 m	2.5 kW
2 x 2 m	1.25 kW	4.2 x 2.4 m	2.7 kW
2.4 x 2 m	1.4 kW	4.8 x 3 m	3.5 kW
3 x 2 m	1.6 kW	5.4 x 3.6 m	4.25 kW

3 How to Deliver the Heat

WARM WATER SYSTEMS

These were in fashion long before any of the more modern systems. They rely on the warmth of water contained in pipes being spread around the greenhouse to give off heat. The water in the pipes can be heated by various means — in a 'boiler' by solid fuel, oil, gas, or electricity. Before dismissing hot water systems too quickly, remember that small bore hot water systems are still the most popular method of heating your dwelling house. This is not simply fashionable, but because they are efficient. Nevertheless while a few enthusiasts remain, gone are the days however when gardeners were prepared to toddle out at all times of the day and night to stoke boilers of the old fashioned soft coal type which were once all the vogue for greenhouses. The 'Clean Air Act' is also a law in most areas, which prohibits the use of soft coal. Boilers have, however, moved with the times and modern oil, gas and solid fuel boilers are of course available. But the high cost of a sophisticated 'automatic' boiler of any type is scarcely likely to be practical for a small greenhouse.

If boilers are to be used for the smaller greenhouse, therefore, they must be of the simpler and cheaper type, which at the end of the day means some work and care.

The real advantage of a pipe system lies in its 'spread' heat around the greenhouse and it is also generally an advantage that the pipes filled with water give off a steady heat which remains for some time after the boiler goes out. The obvious disadvantage is that when the sun suddenly comes out,

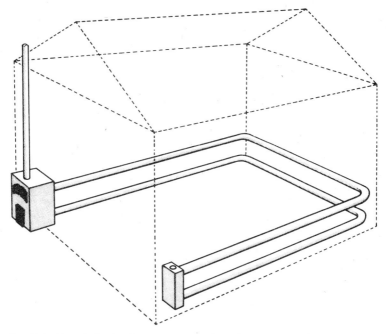

An old fashioned pipe heating system using broad bore pipes

Solid fuel boilers with large bore heating pipes (*courtesy of 'Metomatic'*)

Paraffin fired boiler with hot water pipe system (*courtesy of 'Metomatic'*)

especially in the morning, and the pipes are still hot, this residual heat is not really needed.

Pipe systems are of many varied designs and in small greenhouses invariably work on the principle that hot water rises. This allows the water to circulate naturally from the boiler to the highest point in the system and then return of its own momentum back to the boiler again. If there are to be drops and dips in the pipes, then problems of natural circulation arise and this will mean that a circulating pump is needed, as used in home heating systems, to push the water around. It can be fairly simple to fit pipes or radiators in a lean-to greenhouse and connect up to the home heating system. A problem is, however, that this is generally switched off overnight.

PIPE SIZES

All pipes give off heat according to their diameter as follows:

50 mm approx. 29 W
76 mm approx. 44 W   At 47°C temperature difference
100 mm approx. 58 W   between pipes and air.

24

Fig 29

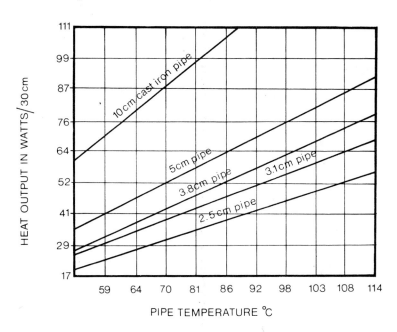

Pipe size table

SOLID FUEL BOILERS

To install a boiler and pipe system there is virtue in having the
boiler unit inside the greenhouse although this is not always
convenient. This ensures maximum use of the radiant heat of
the boiler. A compromise is to have the 'firing' door of the
boiler outside, but the warm back of the boiler inside the
greenhouse. This is a reasonable procedure, especially where
solid fuel is concerned, to avoid the dust and dirt of stoking
the fire in the greenhouse. But a cover should be erected over
the boiler out of doors to avoid excessive draught. The boiler
should be on the north side of the greenhouse, if possible.

With solid fuel systems hopper feeds are available so that the chore of stoking can be largely avoided. But cleaning still remains.

OIL BURNERS

The sophisticated pressure jet and wall flame boiler used in the home is scarcely likely to be used for a small greenhouse. The gardener must turn to vaporiser types of boilers of which several efficient forms are available. All fuels are however becoming more expensive anyway, so do not rush into any system unless it is efficient enough to make good use of your fuel. No electricity is required for simple forms of vaporising burners. Speaking from personal experience I have found that vaporising burners are very easy to operate and economical to run. It is also possible to convert a solid fuel burner to oil with a vaporising burner provided the conversion is done very carefully. The flames are baffled on to the boiler surface or a heat exchanger and the draught for the chimney is reduced as low as possible, otherwise most of your heat will go up the chimney and be wasted.

WASTE OIL BURNERS

There are several types of burners for burning waste car engine oil and one made in Scotland of 3,682 watts burns for 24 hours on 13.6 litre and has a rating of 3,682 watts/21 m of 100 mm pipes. These burners do not require any electricity, which is a distinct point in their favour, and the only real drawback is handling the oil, which can be very messy, and cleaning the burner which can also be an extremely dirty operation, but is essential since this type of fuel has a high waste-matter content and it builds up carbon fairly quickly, which does mean work.

GAS BOILERS

There are several forms of gas boilers suitable for greenhouses and these tend to be much larger than necessary for a small domestic greenhouse. The smallest size is around 5,860 watts and the cost is substantial. Where natural gas supplies are available, many gardeners are turning to Shilton burners for direct siting in the greenhouse.

A modern paraffin fired heater ideal for heating greenhouses where almost all types of crops are being grown. This type of heater is used by commercial growers (*courtesy of Aladdin Industries Ltd*)

CONTROL

Simple solid fuel burners are merely controlled by opening the damper, or adjusting the thermostatic setting controlling this, which allows more or less air to pass through the boiler and up the chimney. This in turn controls the rate of combustion.

With oil fired boilers of simple design there is a control valve which is turned up or down as required, by reference to the greenhouse thermometer.

More sophisticated control operates on an expansion thermostat which returns the boiler to pilot when the boiler reaches the temperature it is set for.

INSTALLATION

Any handyman can quickly install a small or large bore system, especially if a pump is used. For the latter it can be tricky to get pipes threaded for screw joints. Yet this is completely unnecessary as rubber hose with an inside diameter the same as the outside of the pipe, or nearly so, with jubilee clips, can quickly join a system together. For bends all that is necessary is to get 'slow' double 'male' bends and fit the hose over them. One benefit of rubber hose connections is that they allow a fair degree of pipe movement which can be desirable.

RUNNING COSTS

To estimate the cost of any solid fuel boiler, take the cost of the fuel per 100 Kg. Divide by 100 and this gives the cost per Kg. One Kg of solid fuel will average 1,596 watts. All boilers have an efficiency loss, generally 20-25%, so you get on average 1,197 watts per Kg (at the cost calculated). If your boiler is rated at 3,412 watts, then it will burn roughly 450 grams of solid fuel per hour at full output, though full output is seldom necessary.

ELECTRIC WARM AIR FAN HEATERS

There are various sizes available, all of which are simple to use and relatively cheap. Popular sizes are as follows—

    1,250 W
    2,500 W
    3,000 W

Most of these heaters have a built in thermostat (the largest one a thermometer too), which is a control that switches the heating element on or off but allows the fan which pushes air through the element to operate continually. This is certainly useful as it allows the current to circulate the air in the greenhouse whether the heating element is operating or not. Few plants grow well in still air. Fan heaters are usually positioned at the end of the greenhouse opposite the door, with the air stream passing diagonally across the greenhouse. Try to avoid the warm air blowing directly on to the plants.

While warm air is blown out of the heater, raising the air temperature quickly in the vicinity, this does not always mean that the whole greenhouse is uniformly heated. Plants along the outside of the greenhouse can in fact be a lot colder than plants in the vicinity of the heater, especially on a windy night. In practice this is not a serious drawback.

RUNNING COSTS

It is difficult to estimate average running costs for heaters, again much depends on region, tightness of the greenhouse, exposure and other issues. Remember that 1 unit = 1 kW or 3.6 M.J. and that it is necessary to allow for different demands. 10% demand can apply to frost protection only (7°C) in a mild winter. This can rise up to a 60–70% demand in a very cold winter. It will seldom be necessary to operate heat continuously at any level, unless the unit is greatly undersized for the greenhouse in relation to the heat level required by plants in cultivation.

TUBULAR HEATERS (ELECTRICAL)

These useful heaters operate on mains voltage and are fitted to the greenhouse base walls by stout brackets. They contain heating elements in a waterproof case of 5 cm in diameter. They can be used singly or in banks and are rated at 60 watts per 30 cm, which means that you get 1 kW (3.6 M.J.) from 5m. Tubular heaters of the above rating do not get very hot and plants can be grown within a few inches of them quite safely. (Domestic tubular heaters must not be used.)

They are very useful for providing a warm 'curtain' of heat as they can be spread out around the edge of the greenhouse.

Greenhouse fan heater with its own built in thermostat and thermometer
(*courtesy of Humex*)

In this respect they are better than fan heaters. They are, for
safety reasons, best fitted to the base wall of a greenhouse,
although they can readily be installed on the base of wooden
greenhouses. With metal greenhouses they should, again for
safety reasons, be mounted on wooden supports.

OPERATION

This should be through an air thermostat situated in the
greenhouse, preferably out of the way above the bench, which
is set at the desired temperature.

COST TO RUN

This can be calculated in a similar manner to fan heaters,
with the proviso that fan heaters can raise the air temperature
more quickly.

MINERAL INSULATED CABLES (M.I.)

These are useful when a big demand for heat is not necessary.
They are extremely useful for frost protection and are bought
in kits of different loadings. It is a question of obtaining a kit

Tubular heaters are one of the most reliable and economic ways of heating a greenhouse (*courtesy of Humex*)

of the appropriate loading for frost protection. They are secured on special plastic brackets to the base wall of the greenhouse or frame. M.I. cables are used in propagating cases. Note that they should only be used when frost protection operating on an air thermostat set at 7°C and little more is the aim. They are slow to warm up and do not give the quick rise in temperature of a warm air fan heater.

COST TO RUN
Running costs are similar to tubular heaters and should be low if correctly used for frost protection.

CONVECTOR HEATERS

Available in various loadings, these operate by allowing air to enter at the base where it passes over a warm element. Warm air is naturally expelled at the top. The main disadvantage of convector heaters is that unlike fan heaters they tend to give a much more localised heat output. Most have a built-in thermostat, which cannot be as accurate as a fan heater thermostat owing to the build up of heat in the actual thermostat itself, but it is still very useful nevertheless.

Running costs therefore tend to be higher than for fan heaters.

Convector heaters are usually placed in the centre of the greenhouse.

ELECTRIC WATER-FILLED BOILERS

These operate on a thermostatically controlled immersion heater and are made of light gauge galvanised metal with an immersion type heater element. They are in fact like a much enlarged electric kettle.

Like any form of electric space heating other than storage boilers, they tend to be considered expensive in operation. For this reason they are not so popular. Yet they are remarkably accurate and simple to operate. They generally have a built-in thermostat, which ensures maximum economy and quick accurate control of heat. They are available in various sizes.

NIGHT STORE HEATERS

Owing to the problems of temperature control these are not widely used in greenhouses. The more sophisticated forms of storage heaters, i.e. controlled input/output (by fan) would, however, be justified in a conservatory.

Note that it would be necessary to have an off peak current fitted to allow economical operation of night store heaters.

SMALL PARAFFIN HEATERS — burning refined oil (paraffin)

These are basically warm air heating units. A simple circular wick, the base of which is immersed in a reservoir of paraffin, is contained in a metal cylinder. Most are of flueless design. The combination of warm air and carbon dioxide gas which are given off during operation are distributed in various ways to give a fairly large heat output. In addition there are beneficial effects from the carbon dioxide during daylight. Provided the wick is kept clean, free of carbon, and trimmed with scissors to ensure even burning, the obnoxious sulphur content of the oil burned being low (below 0.005%), no harm should befall plants. Few plants, other than some sensitive plants such as primulas, are likely to be adversely affected by the fumes, but there can be build up over a period (especially if vents are kept closed). The 'smell' which one gets from a paraffin heater is not necessarily harmful. Some incorporate a water tray for fume absorption.

On the simple type of heaters the only method of heat control is by adjusting the size of the flame manually, and referring back to a thermometer reading. More sophisticated forms of paraffin heaters have what is called 'module' control. The principle which is involved here is minimal burning rate which is increased when the temperature drops below the thermostatic setting. These burners are most efficient in operation and certainly give maximum economy in use from what has now become an expensive fuel. Later types are much more sophisticated.

OPERATION

To set up and operate paraffin heaters it is necessary of course to refer to the instructions supplied with them. Simplicity is, however, the keynote. Maintenance involves cleaning and filling.

Placement of the heaters in the centre of the greenhouse floor is usual. In a very 'tight' greenhouse it is always advisable to leave a ventilator very slightly open to allow the necessary air for combustion. It also helps to allow any obnoxious fumes to escape.

These heaters are available in many sizes and the rating is stated in watts per hour. Popular sizes are between 3,000 and 9,000 W. This is again related to the calculated heat loss of the greenhouse. Some firms, on completion of a form, are happy to give heat load requirements involved on a comparative regional basis. Consumption per hour is also stated with the heater in question.

RUNNING COSTS

It is simple to make calculations. Fuel oil averages approximately 10,325 watts per litre, and allowing for the inevitable loss of efficiency in burning, one gets 7,000 W or slightly more of actual heat. Thus a 700 W output burner will give 10 hours burning at full output per litre. As full consumption is seldom necessary, considerably longer will be achieved.

The rising price of fuel oil has tended to make paraffin heaters a less attractive proposition than a year or so ago. The same general rules can be applied to all oil burners.

SOLAR HEAT UNITS

So far these are only in the early stages of development for domestic and other buildings. They can take several forms, including the use of heat pumps, but it is unlikely that there will be much development for amateur greenhouse use within the next year or two.

A point to note, however, is that the rear wall of a south facing lean-to greenhouse or conservatory can act as a wonderful reservoir of heat. The same is true of concrete paths or floors.

GAS HEATERS (Flueless)

Until the advent of natural gas there was little interest in gas for greenhouse heating, the exception to this of course being the hot water pipe system where the boiler was heated by gas (town or natural). Propane burners have been available for a long while and were always a perfectly acceptable form of greenhouse heating, apart from the higher cost of buying gas in containers.

Town gas could never be used for direct heating in flueless appliances owing to its impurities, especially sulphur, which were harmful to the growing plants. With the advent of natural gas, however, the situation has completely changed. The *Shilton* burner particularly has made a big impact in amateur greenhouse heating. Fitted at least 3 inches from a

The Shilton Gas Heater (*courtesy of Humex*)

wall or side of the greenhouse and at least 6 inches below any staging, these heaters are complete with a flexible pipe for connecting up to a gas supply which must be **installed by a qualified pipe fitter.** The burners are fitted with thermostat or flame failure device for safety. There are two sizes, the 1500 which has a rating of 1,500 watts and the 2700 which has a rating of 2,500 watts. Their fitting is simple and in practice they are economical to run, especially if you are already on a high useage for domestic consumption. Details of tariffs can be obtained by contacting your local Gas Board.

POINTS TO NOTE IN THE USE OF GAS BURNERS

Air is required to burn any fuel. The 'leak' in any greenhouse is usually quite sufficient to allow the necessary entry of air. In a plastic greenhouse, however, there could be problems. It will be found that condensation is greater (compared to electric heaters) when gas is used, due to the combustion process.

A particularly valuable side issue with natural gas, however, is the release of carbon dioxide, which adds to the initial quantities present in the atmosphere and which plants ' use for manufacturing food in their leaves.

Gas can be used for firing boilers linked to pipe systems or as warm air units.

Portable propane burners can of course be used for greenhouse heating, the main disadvantage being the running costs which tend to be rather high, although with the high cost of oil they are now coming into their own.

4 Cooling Your Greenhouse

The ventilation of greenhouses is something far too many of us take for granted, forgetting that we can just as easily 'cook' our plants in summer as we can freeze them in winter.

Ventilation means allowing the entry of cooler fresh air from outside the greenhouse to replace 'stale' and often overheated air of the inside of the greenhouse.

The air in the greenhouse becomes warm because the sun's rays passing through the glass are absorbed and reflected by plants, paths and benches, so heating the air. The rays of the sun cause plants to lose moisture rapidly or transpire by warming them physically. This lost moisture quickly turns into vapour, making the air very moist or muggy. While both heat and moisture are obviously desirable to a certain degree, an excess of both is undesirable for all but a few plants —plants which few people are likely to want to grow anyway.

Remember that most plants breathe all the time and manufacture food in their leaves continuously **during daylight**. To do this most plants must have constant supplies of **fresh** air.

VENTILATION

What ventilation really adds up to is allowing or forcing the overheated stale and often moist air to leave the greenhouse and bring in suitable quantities of cooler, drier, fresh air from outside.

It is indeed fortunate that air, being a gas, rises when it gets warm. In the case of a conventionally shaped greenhouse it rises to the highest point of the roof. If there is a suitable outlet or ventilator at the highest point, this allows the hot air to escape. Fresh air comes into the greenhouse to a certain extent in competition with the air going out by interchange, which varies in rate according to the size of the ventilator and how windy it is out of doors. Cool air (being heavier than hot air) can also be taken in by side or low set vents and doors. It also makes quite a difference if your ventilators are on the windy side of the greenhouse so that they catch or scoop the cool air and deflect this around the greenhouse. Things can get really critical when the weather is very warm, windless and sunny and the hot air in the greenhouse cannot escape or new air gain entry quickly enough for various reasons. The result is that the greenhouse becomes overheated, and an overheated greenhouse can kill plants really rapidly.

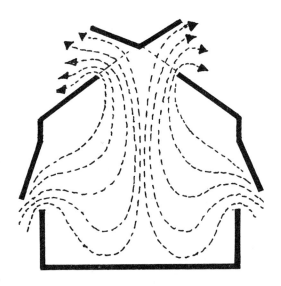

An efficient ventilation system based on the principle that hot air rises. Cold air comes in through the side windows while hot air escapes through the roof vents

Size of Ventilators   The actual size of the ventilators should be related to the size of the greenhouse. For a 6 x 8 foot greenhouse covering 48 square feet of ground area it is necessary to have at least 16 square feet of vent area. For really efficient ventilation this means four 2 x 2 foot ventilators. If only two are fitted, as is often the case, the greenhouse will become excessively hot during very sunny weather, unless the door is considered as part of the ventilation area which it often is.

If, however, louvre or hinged vents in the side walls are also fitted, this allows additional cool air to gain entry, which speeds up the whole ventilating process. The doors also serve for this purpose.

If ventilators are not set in the highest point of the roof, a layer of hot air is trapped in the apex.

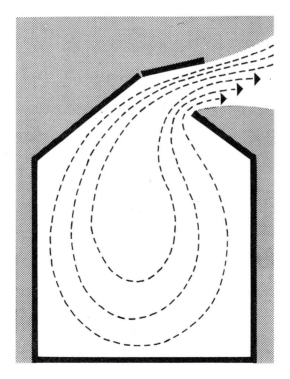

The relatively slow moving air circulation in a greenhouse with a single vent

Fans Fans can also be used to **extract** hot air, provided there is a sufficient size of inlet to allow in fresh air. In domestic greenhouses it is usual to have the fan at one gable end and the inlet at the other, although sometimes they are fitted in the roof. The size of the fan and its capacity are

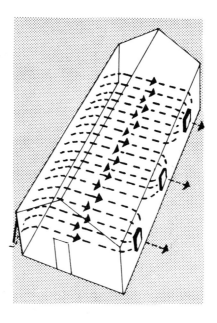

Fan ventilation, commonly used by commercial growers, is the most efficient system of all. Most plants like air circulating round them.

critical and here are the average specifications for fans in greenhouses, along with inlet size.

(Catalogues usually give fan sizes based on air changes per hour, the normal figure being 30, so be sure that the information gives you the details of fan sizes.)

Greenhouse cubic capacity	Air changes per hour
360 cu. ft	40
425 cu. ft	34
670 cu. ft	21
1100 cu. ft	13

Fans can be used to pull fresh air out of the garden and put it into the greenhouse, where it is extracted through vents. In practice the extraction fan is the better arrangement. Other fans can be used simply to mix the air in the greenhouse.

OPERATION OF VENTILATORS AND FANS

Ventilators The heat level from the sun is never constant for long. This results in constantly changing temperatures in the greenhouse. As the amount a ventilator is open controls the exit and entry of air, it is difficult to provide the even temperature which most plants respond to by opening or closing ventilators manually following frequent reference to a thermometer, unless you are prepared to camp in the greenhouse.

One simple way of overcoming this is to fit expansion type vent lifts which open and close automatically according to prevailing temperatures. Other systems, dependent on electric motors are available for opening ventilators automatically but are more costly to install.

Vent lifts of the expansion type are available in different sizes according to the size of ventilator involved. It is usual to fit them only to the roof vents, operating side vents by hand, although they can be fitted to both.

Fans Fans are operated by electricity, so a separate thermostat is the simplest way of achieving their operation. This starts and stops the fan according to the temperature recorded by the thermostat which is the converse of a heating thermostat. The inlet for the fans is best left open slightly or half open, according to whether the fans are likely to be operating only occasionally or often. Louvre type inlets are useful.

A still further way of cooling the greenhouse is as discussed previously by pulling air into the greenhouse with a fan. It is discharged through louvre type outlets which can be adjusted to open automatically when the fan comes on. Such systems are available from specialist manufacturers and can be obtained with heaters incorporated.

It is worth remembering that no greenhouse is completely tight and that there is always a degree of inadvertent ventilation through cracks in glass, doors, and so on, so some ventilation takes place all the time.

The Autofan provides one of the most efficient of greenhouse ventilation systems (*courtesy of Humex*)

An air circulator causes a continual movement of air in the greenhouse which is necessary for plants to grow healthily (*courtesy of Humex*)

LEAN-TO GREENHOUSES OR CONSERVATORIES

The ventilation of lean-to greenhouses poses special ventilation problems for several reasons. Where they face south (and they usually do) the large area of glass presented to the sun allows maximum transmission of sun heat. There is also the problem of the wall behind the lean-to greenhouse absorbing a lot of heat and throwing this back into the greenhouse to take into account. With a lean-to greenhouse there is only one side available for the fitting of ridge vents, and this can restrict exit of warm air.

Where greenhouses are of three quarter span and the top of the greenhouse is above the top of the wall, ventilation can be more efficient, as this allows vents on both sides of the ridge.

It is best in all lean-to greenhouses or conservatories to have front vents as well as roof vents. While these help, overheating frequently occurs since it is impossible to encourage sufficient air exchange. Fan ventilation is frequently the only way of ventilating a lean-to structure effectively. It is usual to fit the fan at one end and allow entry at the other.

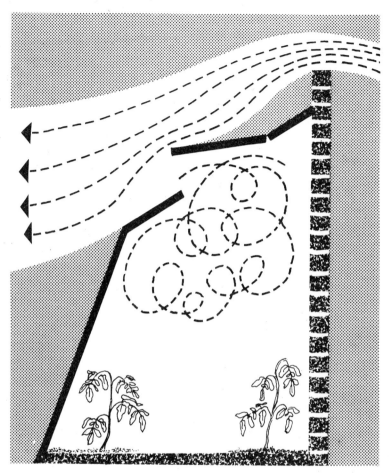

Lean-to greenhouses are the most difficult of all to ventilate since hot air tends to linger in the upper regions of the lean-to

PLASTIC GREENHOUSES

There is always a lot of condensation in plastic greenhouses, so that crops can be spoiled. Ventilation is therefore especially important. With small polythene greenhouses leaving ends open will usually allow adequate ventilation but there are problems and the polythene covering is considered expendable, circular holes can be cut in the sides after June, using a dustbin lid and a razor blade.

BLINDS AND SHADING

Ventilation is only one aspect of cooling a greenhouse. Shading is another. The two should ideally be interrelated since both serve the same basic purpose. They both reduce the effect of the heat from the very hot sun, which in turn reduces the temperature of the greenhouse during sunny weather in the summer, with of course a considerable saving in the frequency of watering and avoidance of plants being cooked.

The simplest form of shading is to paint on white or green material on the outside of the glass, preferably to reflect sunlight in the late spring. By winter, when all available light is required, the shading material will usually have been washed off by rain. Much diluted emulsion paint, lime plus water, or green shading material can all be used. It may only be necessary to shade the southern aspect of the greenhouse.

▲ Greenhouse blinds. The sun visors are one of the most efficient methods of
◀ shading a greenhouse yet invented. A patented system holds the blinds rigid
at the correct slope of the roof of the greenhouse. The blinds can be operated
automatically by an electronic eye (*courtesy of Humex*)

A new type of shading goes on the outside of the glass, going transparent when wet, which it often is in winter, so does not need to be removed.

The real usefulness of shading can be seen to best effect for many pot plants such as busy Lizzies or begonias, which can scorch badly in the sun.

Roller shades can be obtained for either the outside or the inside of the greenhouse. In the former case they are largely of cedar wood or plastic and are used mainly by orchid, fern or alpine gardeners. But roller shading can be used inside the greenhouse to very good effect as required. Better still, the shades can be operated automatically by thermostat or, in a still more sophisticated way, by light cell or magic eye. Shade blinds of any kind can be obtained from specialist suppliers who issue full instructions on their installation. Green polyethylene or plastic mesh material can be used as a temporary measure, supported by canes or wires.

Venetian blinds type shading can also be used and is additionally useful in winter for giving extra insulation against loss of heat, or conversely the entry of frost. They can also be

Roller blinds provide one of the simplest methods of shading a greenhouse manually (*courtesy of Humex*)

closed or opened automatically by thermostat or electric eye.

Shading has applications other than keeping hot sun from the plants. It can be especially useful in cases where disease is present in plants such as tomatoes suffering from wilt diseases, to make the atmosphere muggy.

To obtain any kind of blinds it is necessary to contact the manufacturer giving exact dimensions and type of greenhouse and other related information.

Cooling of the greenhouse can also be brought about by spraying water down the outside of the glass, following the old butchers' window idea. To do this it is necessary to have a submersible pump in a reservoir of water connected up to a perforated hose running along the outside ridge of the greenhouse. The water is collected in the gutters and returned to the tank. The operation of the pump is controlled by a thermostat inside the greenhouse. Reductions of 5-6°C are possible by this method, especially if the water is coloured with green dye.

46

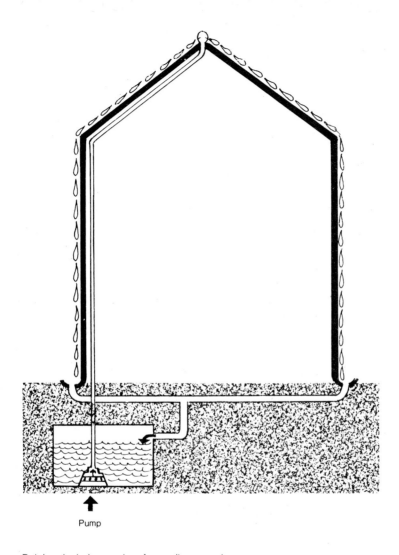

Pump

Butchers' window system for cooling greenhouses

5 Watering, Feeding and Staging

Perhaps the biggest single chore in any greenhouse is the application of water — knowing how much to give and when to give it, and more important still remembering to apply it. This is because all the water which plants in a greenhouse require must be supplied by the gardener — as opposed to plants in the garden, where you can usually leave watering to the rain. The possible exception to this is when water seeps in through the greenhouse foundations from outside and plants are being grown in the greenhouse border, which is not a particularly good thing, especially in winter.

There is also the important business of supplying the plants with their necessary food, something else which lies almost entirely in the gardener's hands, since starved plants are scarcely likely to crop or flower as well as they should. Fortunately the advent of simple-to-use, safe and easy-to-apply liquid fertilizers can make watering and feeding a simultaneous process.

WATER SUPPLIES

A tap with a good supply of fresh, clean water from the mains (or better still through the domestic supply tank) is essential, since nothing could be worse than running around carrying water in cans or buckets. Where a greenhouse is not in use at all during the winter there can be problems of freezing up, unless the water can be shut off without shutting off the house supply. For this reason many gardeners still prefer to take their water into the greenhouse with a hose from a water tap in a nearby garage or shed.

Hoses and Cans   The simplest way to water plants is to slosh water around from a hose pipe, which is all right for tomatoes and cucumbers growing in borders but not very clever with pots or boxes.

Tanks   A tank is a useful piece of equipment in any greenhouse. Indoor plastic water tanks with removable tops are ideal (if water is kept dark lest algae or other growth will develop.) A suitably sized tank is 15-20 gallons, placed in an odd corner. Under a bench is quite a good position, provided there is still easy access for a watering can and things do not drop into it. However, there are automatic systems which are definitely to be preferred, both from yours and from the plants' point of view.

Spray Lines   These are available for suspending above growing plants such as tomatoes or lettuce, when water is applied over the crop in a fine mist. All that is necessary is to link up a hose pipe to the end of the spray line and provided there is sufficient pressure and volume of water, out comes the mist. Don't be fooled by volume of water. You may think you have a good supply until you find that your spray line only produces water from the end two nozzles. The answer is a supply pipe of larger diameter from an unrestricted main. The crop is drenched under a fine mist and the surplus water drips on to the soil. Spray lines water a crop with remarkable evenness if they are operating well. Their one drawback is that once a crop such as tomatoes gets a little tall, the plants can be too wet if watered overhead, which in turn can start off fungal troubles. Spray lines can, however, be lowered once the lower fruit is taken from the plants, whether this is tomatoes or cucumbers.

Trickle and Drip Lines   These can take several forms. A popular form is where separate tubes go into each pot or seed pan from the main pipe. Other forms merely use perforated lines or lay-flat polythene, when the water comes out in fine jet form. In both cases it is necessary to connect up the trickle or drip lines to a suitably handy supply, high pressure not being needed. No really totally satisfactory equipment can be

49

Trickle lines are a fairly workable system for watering individual plants in the home greenhouse

used to control these systems owing to the range of crops being grown. I prefer to use mine manually by referring to a moisture meter in the soil, although a slowly filling tank system is available for supplying gravel trays and individual plants.

Capillary Benches These can be bought in kit form or can be put together by the handyman gardener. A well constructed strong bench with three raised sides and completely level is lined with polythene and then filled with sand. Coarse sand is used for the bottom ¼ inch, then fine sand to give 2-3 inch total depth. Down the middle a plastic tube or hose pipe perforated every few inches is laid on top or below the sand. More sophisticated systems can be bought complete with all equipment. There are various means to control water level — either a ball cock tank to give a controlled water level ½-1 inch below the level of the sand or a float controller or valve.

The plants on top of the capillary bench, preferably in plastic trays or plastic pots, obtain their water by suction. Even a polythene lined bench topped up every day with water from a hose is a lot better than nothing, although what can happen is that the bench becomes too dry and the roots penetrate too far into it. This can mean a severe check when the plants are lifted. More recently and very successfully fibre glass sheeting is used on top of polythene.

50

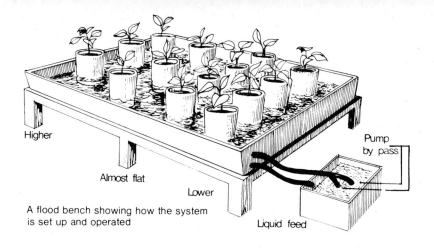

Higher

Almost flat

Lower

A flood bench showing how the system
is set up and operated

Pump
by pass

Liquid feed

Header tank designed to supply water to a trickle irrigation line

Another system is called the flood bench, which is a bench with high sides, lined with polythene, and flooded to a depth of 3 inches or so. From a tank the water is then allowed to drain away gradually and pumped back to the tank. This can be done on the slowly filling ball cock valve system. Green algae grow on all capillary systems, but although unsightly, do no harm.

Gravel Trays Here plastic trays filled with gravel are used to. stand plants on. They give the plants humidity and water by capillary pull. They are perhaps more useful in the home where the atmosphere is dry rather than in the greenhouse. Fibre glass mats can also be used in them in lieu of gravel.

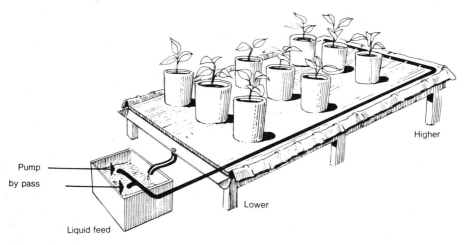

Flow bench system of watering on a greenhouse bench

Flow Bench A new form of hydroponics is the flow bench, where shallow benches are lined with polythene, level across the axis, with a gradual slope in one direction. They are then lined with an absorbent matting material. By means of a tank, a submersible pump and plastic piping, a continuous flow of dissolved nutrient is sent through the bench. Plants in plastic pots are placed on the bench, where they pull up water and nutrients as required. This is an ideal system for the pot plant grower who is away from a home a lot on business. The nutrient solution is changed every 2-3 weeks.

Dilutors Plastic dilutors operate by displacement. They automatically mix liquid foods with water, avoiding a lot of careful measuring. They are connected up to a hose pipe **but the water supply must not be directly from the main supply. This is not permitted by water authorities as it can allow contamination of water supplies.** In addition varying pressures can of course affect the dilutor. Many gardeners simply prefer to mix up the liquid feeds as required, either in the watering can or in a barrel. If all the diluted liquid feed in a barrel is not used and more liquid feed is added, the dilution is obviously not correct. In time this could result in damage to plants or poor results.

I referred earlier to the need to decide how much water your

Wick system for watering greenhouse plants

plants require and in the unit growing a range of odds and ends there is unfortunately no real substitute for judgement. The obvious answer for a mixed batch of pot plants is some form of capillary bench.

LOOKING AFTER YOUR PLANTS AT HOLIDAY TIME

Capillary benches, especially if supplied automatically by float controller or other means, are especially useful at holiday time. Flow benches are also ideal for the holiday period for bench grown plants. Other systems operating for border grown or container grown plants are seldom likely to be operated automatically, but can be to a limited extent with the slowly filling tank system. Pot plants can of course be plunged in wet peat or can be put in a container of any kind. Wads of tape can be led out of the pots into a reservoir of water and this works reasonably well. The root ball must be knocked out of the pot and the tape then inserted and led out of the drainage hole, which may require enlarging.

Often, however, there is no substitute for the help of a gardening friend, provided you do likewise when he or she goes off on holiday.

Many gardeners are in doubt about how much water to give plants, it being easy to over-water some plants such as geraniums and underwater others like fuchsia. A little moisture meter is a good gadget for helping you here, but take time and trouble to check up whether the plants themselves like it dry or wet before giving water on a routine basis.

BENCHES

Benches in greenhouses are necessary for pot plants, general seed sowing, propagation, and for generally avoiding the strain of bending, and bringing plants up to the light. Benches can in fact be in tiers, the highest level being very useful in the winter months.

Benches are not required for 'border' growing of plants in the ground — such as tomatoes, lettuce, chrysanthemums, cucumbers and the like. A compromise is to have removable benches which can be taken out after the early propagation activities are past to allow the use of the border.

Benches can be of various heights, usually around 30 inches, and must be of a width in keeping with the greenhouse. It is bad policy to make benches too wide, not more than about 3-3ft 6in — otherwise it becomes difficult to reach to the back.

Benches made of aluminium or steel are provided by green-

Wire mesh benches of this type are ideal for plants watered by trickle systems since they allow for fully free drainage

A capillary watering system
(*courtesy of Humex*)

house manufacturers. Alternatively they can be made up simply with angle iron, with expanded metal or wooden slats or entirely from wood. These materials allow open type benches. Solid benches can be made up with corrugated asbestos or corrugated iron (asbestos lasts longer but is more brittle). Solid wood can also be used but tends to rot.

At all events benches must be solidly constructed, especially for mist propagation units or capillary benches. The combined weight of propagation units plus plants in pots can be very considerably and any collapse occurring during the season could be disastrous.

Always leave a space between the bench and the outside of the greenhouse to allow passage of heat when pipes or tubular electric heating systems are involved.

PLASTIC GREENHOUSES
You may have decided that instead of an ordinary greenhouse made of wood, alloy, steel and *glass* you want one of the many types of plastic structures available. You will find it a lot cheaper to buy, the reason being, of course, that the plastic has a limited life.

A plastic greenhouse will basically be the same as an ordinary greenhouse, but you will find it more costly to heat on average and more difficult to ventilate. It will also be a lot more humid and muggy due to condensation, which although a good thing for some crops, could give rise to problems with tomatoes and other plants which do not like excessive dampness, especially overnight. Support can also be a problem. Plastic greenhouses must be securely anchored down or they can blow away under windy conditions.

CROP SUPPORT
Something which is frequently overlooked is the need for crop support, particularly when growing tomatoes or cucumber. You will also need support for vines, peaches and nectarines if you aspire to that sort of thing.

Strong galvanised steel wires are generally stretched along the length of the greenhouse, 2-2½ feet apart for tomatoes and cucumbers, and on the sides and roof 9-12 inches apart for peaches, nectarines and vines. With a wooden greenhouse

Crop support systems, suitable for tomatoes, grape vines, melons and so on

hooks or 'eyes' can readily be screwed into the wood, but with alloy greenhouses it may be necessary to obtain special brackets from the manufacturer or bore a few holes here and there. Most manufacturers are thoughtful enough to provide crop support facilities these days.

6 Controlling Your Greenhouse Environment

Many gardeners would be very happy simply to open or close ventilators when they think necessary, generally as little as possible, and switch on and off heaters in cold weather as required. A lot of gardeners are obviously not in the least interested in any degree of automation because they cannot see the real benefit. Apart from this all gadgets cost money, which is a consideration. But to be practical consider things this way.

Automatic ventilation, usually with expansion vents which lift the ventilators up and down, is the first simple step, and look at the great advantage of having vents which open and shut automatically according to the temperature of the greenhouse. If you like, of course, fans can be installed to operate automatically on a thermostat. If you automatically control your heating you will end up saving a lot of money, having spent a little extra to begin with.

Thermostatic control of electric heaters is especially economic. Most of them in fact having a built-in thermostat anyway. If they have not, which may be the case with tubular heaters or M.I. cables, then you will need a separate thermostat. But this is still money well spent because no one can determine what is going to happen to the outside temperature in advance. It may be a lovely mild night when you go off to bed and then you wake up to find a solid white frost which can ruin months of work in plant or seed raising.

Paraffin heaters and their control have been discussed elsewhere, as also has the means of controlling coal and oil fired boilers, and while there are some difficulties in

A plastic greenhouse

achieving complete automatic control, all ideas are worth exploring.

The barrier to obtaining precise control of oil and coal fired boilers serving a hot water pipe system frequently lies in their simple design, which has been necessary to keep cost down. Where it is possible to utilise a more sophisticated coal or oil boiler in conjunction with home heating, these problems largely disappear, apart from night control when the domestic system is generally out of action on a time clock basis. The way out here is to site the boiler in the greenhouse or conservatory if possible, which can as we have discussed give further problems during daytime operation of the boiler for domestic purposes on a hot day.

Gas boilers for domestic heating, again sited in the greenhouse or conservatory, offer the same trouble. Where a gas boiler is used specifically for greenhouse heating, either a Shilton burner or gas boiler linked to a pipe system, problems of control seldom exist due to the necessary thermostatic control essential with all gas burning appliances.

The same precise control can of course be obtained with a sophisticated oil burner for the greenhouse.

Control of bench warming is readily achieved by use of a thermostat, as described in Chapter 7 and there has also been discussion on mist units and their control. Watering systems and their operation has also been referred to in Ch. 5 and certainly the capillary bench system for pot plant culture offers the most foolproof method of automatic control. Blinds can readily be operated by magic eye but are more usually operated manually.

Humidity control is possible but is difficult to achieve. Humidistats are like thermostats but they operate at a given degree of moisture content in the air, not temperature. Whilst they can be used, it is a problem to decide what they should actually control. Do they put on the heating, open the vents or operate fans? Or do they put spraylines into operation if the greenhouse is too dry? It is possible, if a humidistat is installed, to link this on to fan ventilation to take over or override the normal thermostat for operating the fans to restore the moisture content of the air, but there are still many problems with this type of equipment.

RANGE OF INSTRUMENTS

Thermostats These switch off or on electric power to various pieces of equipment. They can be set to do this at various temperatures. The rod type thermostat is generally used for greenhouse work. Room types are sometimes used, especially in aspirated screens.

To get the best out of any thermostat it should be sheltered from the hot sun or draughts, otherwise it can give false readings. They will seldom in fact ever give a true reading unless they are put in what is called an aspirated screen. Remember that a separate thermostat will be required for operating fans, one which comes on as the temperature rises, *not off* as the heating thermostat will do.

Aspirated Screens A vital issue with all instruments, which includes thermometers and thermostats, is the way they are shaded from hot sun or draughts. Here an insulated box of some type houses the relevant instruments and a small constantly running fan continuously pulls air over them. It is unfortunate that few manufacturers offer aspirated screens for the amateur because they are a really good investment.

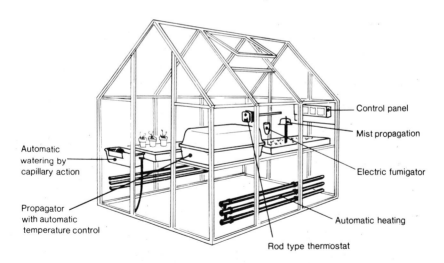

Control panel

Mist propagation

Automatic watering by capillary action

Electric fumigator

Propagator with automatic temperature control

Automatic heating

Rod type thermostat

Diagram showing how just about every aspect of greenhouse management can be automated

Thermometers   These take several forms and vary from ones simply recording temperatures to the maximum/minimum re-set types. These latter types are valuable as they allow some checking back on how high or low the temperature has actually been during a given period.

Hygrometers   These tell the humidity of the air in the greenhouse, which is useful information even if not a great deal can sometimes be done about moisture content.

Moisture Meters   These come in various forms and can be used to check the moisture content of the soil in pots or benches.

Time Clocks   can be used to give specified periods of fan ventilation or lighting at night.

CARBON DIOXIDE ENRICHMENT

There has been a lot of publicity about artificial enrichment of the atmosphere of the greenhouse with extra carbon dioxide gas. The idea is to stimulate plants to grow more quickly by giving them an extra supply of carbon dioxide gas to use for the food manufacturing process called photosynthesis which goes on in the leaves during daylight. The use of flueless paraffin and gas heaters enriches the air of the greenhouse with carbon dioxide considerably!

Due to the difficulty of checking the exact concentration of carbon dioxide in the air, it is not really practical for gardeners to purposely set out to enrich the greenhouse air, except by the use of heaters.

The use of organic matter in the soil and the use of straw bales for tomato or cucumber culture results in considerable production of carbon dioxide, with beneficial effects to the plants.

PEST AND DISEASE CONTROL

Keeping a greenhouse clean is important and it should always be washed down at least once a year. This also applies to receptacles. Dealing with pests and disease outbreaks is a lot simpler these days with the range of chemicals available and sprayers to apply them, including electric fumigators. Makers' directions should always be followed closely with all materials.

7 Soil and Bench Warming

The purpose of soil or bench warming is, as the name implies, to impart warmth locally in the root area of the plants. It is by no means a new technique and has in fact, in various guises, been around for countless years. No wonder, since it is sound common sense to put heat *exactly* where you want it. It saves you money too.

Probably the greatest exponents were the French with their hot bed system of culture, called *Terreaux*. Here fermenting manure was used, with soil heaped on top, warmed by the manure to grow early crops under the protection of cold frames, bell jars, hand lights and other devices. Although there may still be some enthusiasts who carry out soil warming by the use of manure, I haven't met many in recent years, so it is a practice which has slipped out of popularity for various reasons. Not least of these is the difficulty of obtaining regular and reliable supplies of farmyard manure. Perhaps the only revival of the technique is the straw bale system of tomato and cucumber culture. Here fermenting straw is a wonderfully cheap way of providing warmth at the roots (see *The Complete Book of the Greenhouse* — I.G.Walls)

On the maxim of warm toes, cool heads, it has been realised for a long time that plants will grow better with a warmer soil or growing mix in the root area than is the case under normal culture which relies on air heating. Tomato roots, for example, continue to grow better up to about 24°C and cucumbers up to 27°C. If you think about it, this is why tomatoes will always grow well near the heater or boiler. Remember also that once the heat builds up in pots or borders it is retained more readily. This is in contrast to the air of a greenhouse, the temperature of which rises and falls very rapidly according to changing conditions. This you can check fairly quickly with a soil thermometer and an air thermometer, and compare readings over a period.

WAYS OF WARMING SOILS AND BENCHES

Nurserymen have found several ways of effectively warming either growing borders or benches. These involve either warm water filled alkathene pipes of 2 inch diameter in borders at 9-12 in depth or the placement of small bore steel pipes (1½-2 inches in diameter) **on** the actual growing borders. None of these methods, other than perhaps the nearness of warm water filled heating pipes on the growing border or bench are really practical in a small greenhouse. There are, however, some methods which are.

Soil Warming Electric cables, which become warm by resistance of the electrical current passing through them, are a very practical and economic way of warming either borders or benches. For this, use sheathed mains voltage cables. To use them first measure up the border (or frame) in question and obtain a soil warming kit of the appropriate size. The soil is dug out to a depth of 9 inches and the cables are laid in at the appropriate distance apart. This is usually about 5-6 inches, to give a loading of 6-7 watts per square foot. The cables can be kept in position by small bent bits of wire (hair pins if you like) before the soil is replaced. An easy to remember loading is 1 kW for 150 square feet, which shows how economic soil warming can be. 150 square feet after all is a large area, and this can be fully heated for one hour by one unit.

We will discuss the control of temperature later.

Bench Warming Here is one of the most economic and best possible ways of achieving excellent results with a wide range of growing activities with minimum cost and work and it is really so easy to do that anyone can do it in no time. The make-up of the bench is shown in the figures. Once again sufficient cable is allowed for the requisite bench size. For all purposes (except mist propagation) the loading is 7·5 watts per square foot. A 1 kW (1000 watt) unit will therefore warm a very considerable area, and for this reason cables are made up in smaller loading. A 75-watt unit will warm 10 square feet of bench, say 5 x 2 feet. This shows once again how economic they are in operation. The use of polythene tents or drapes over the bench, which would cost only a few pence, further localises the heat and shows precisely what can readily be done at negligible cost. With both soil and bench warming installed, the desirable temperature can be achieved in the minimum of time and with no worry at all without depending on air warmth.

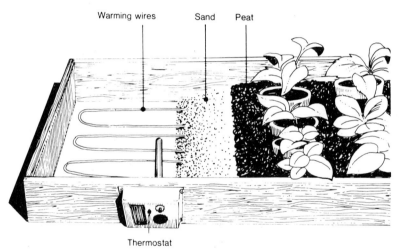

Soil warming cables suitable for bench warming or plant propagation

Control   There are three methods of controlling soil or bench warming units.
1) At 'off peak' tariff through a special meter which the Electricity Board may supply, to give approximately eight hours operation in each 24. You may have an off peak circuit in the home, which makes things a lot easier.
2) Manual switching on and off according to weather, by checking soil or bench warmth with a soil thermometer (this applies especially to border warming). Frames out of doors

can be operated by a thermostat. Although this may sound tedious it is not too big a job, provided you do remember to do it.

3) Best of all perhaps by the use of an 18 inch rod or phial and capillary tube thermostat set across the cable, across the run of the wires but below the surface of the soil or sand. If, in the case of a bench, the space between pots or boxes is filled with peat, this allows for still more efficient operation and minimises the time that the system will be called into action by the thermostat.

Thermostats are provided by the suppliers of soil/bench warming cables.

Note: To avoid accidents, it is essential to switch off soil or bench warming systems before using metal tools. It is also essential to ensure that you have a properly earthed electrical point and connection, and that you only use cables with an earth screen as an integral part of the cable. This ensures that the fuse will 'blow' if the cable is damaged.

A few other points worth noting. When considering soil warmed benches especially, the weight of wet sand must be taken into account, ensuring that benches are strongly constructed, otherwise you could have a real disaster. Check that all wiring conforms to rigid safety standards, using waterproof fittings throughout. It is perfectly practical (and not always realised) that self-watering capillary benches can be combined with bench warming, a matter which is discussed later.

USE OF SOIL BENCH WARMING AND ITS PRACTICAL APPLICATION IN CROP CULTURE

Soil Warming Soil warming installations are especially useful for warmth loving crops such as tomatoes and cucumbers to avoid checks to the roots by cold soil. All that is necessary is to switch on the system some 48 hours before planting is intended. The temperature of the soil at 5in depth is then checked to see that it is at least 13°C for tomatoes and 16°C for cucumbers. For lettuce 7°C is adequate. Note, however, that air temperatures must also be of a reasonably commensurate level. It is folly, for example, to have a root warmth of 13°C and an air temperature of 10°C. Unless you have air heating with fan heaters or other means, this will mean waiting until the weather is sufficiently warm, otherwise you could have problems.

Lettuce are an extremely useful crop to grow with soil warming cables as they can tolerate very low air temperatures, and this is true of many other crops.

A little experience of soil/bench warming growing soon illustrates their value in practical terms. The figures illustrate this point still further, when it can be seen that a small rise in air temperature raises the consumption of electricity considerably in a 6 x 8 foot greenhouse with a brick base wall over a year's average use, as follows:

$$4°C \ x \text{ units}$$

$$7°C \ 2x \text{ units}$$

$$10°C \ 3 \cdot 5x \text{ units}$$
$$13°C \ 5 \cdot 5x \text{ units}$$
$$16°C \ 7 \cdot 5x \text{ units}$$

8 Mist Propagation

This is perhaps more for the enthusiast than for the beginner but if you are really keen on growing things such as shrubs or trees from cuttings, a small mist unit could be a great money saver. Originally devised in the U.S.A. and then further developed in Britain, the fundamental object of mist propagation is to supply moisture by a fine spray of water to keep the leaves of cuttings moist and cool. In many ways the principles are the same as using a propagating case. The difference is that a constant film of moisture is maintained on the plants by mist jets and not by high humidity in the air. By so doing, you can remove many of the problems associated with propagating cases where very soft leaves often tend to rot or be invaded by all sorts of undesirable moulds, fungi, bacteria and so on.

Hose pipes or watering cans fitted with a fine rose can, I suppose, achieve exactly the same effect, provided you are prepared to hose over the plants frequently night and day, which is obviously impractical however keen a greenhouse gardener you may be.

SOIL WARMING

Mist propagation is at its best when used in conjunction with electric (or other method) soil warming cables, to give loading of 15 watts per square foot. Owing to the large amount of water sprayed on the plants, it is important that when the bench is made up drainage is perfect. If not, the bench becomes saturated, which will greatly slow up the whole rooting process.

EQUIPMENT NECESSARY

Mist propagation kits can be bought. These involve nozzles of 15-24 inches high, which are spaced apart at a distance of 3-4 feet according to water pressure. The water pressure should ideally be between 40 and 60 p.s.i. and if this is not possible then a pressure tank will be required. Your Water Board or a plumber will advise you about water pressure.

ELECTRONIC 'LEAVES' OR DETECTORS

The leaf which controls the operation of a valve, starts and stops the supply of water to the mist nozzles. The leaf can take various forms and suppliers of equipment are aware of the best type for a particular district. They generally operate on the evaporation or absorbent principle, and before you dismiss this as being too technical, think about it a little. Quite simply the water evaporates from leaves of the cuttings at the same rate as it does from the artificial leaf or detector, as it would after watering or when it rains out of doors. At a certain point of evaporation this sets off the water spray again for a short burst. When the moisture film is restored the water is shut off, which is quite simple and straightforward really. Light cells can also be obtained to operate mist units, but are not in such general use as electronic type leaves.

Other equipment includes control box, strainers, solenoid valves and short pipes and nozzles.

An electricity supply is required for operating all forms of artificial leaf, as of course it is for electric soil warming equipment.

NEED FOR WEANING

Cuttings become rooted with amazing speed under ideal conditions of good light, warmth and moisture, especially if they are in 50/50 peat/coarse sand rooting medium. It is best if the cuttings are in boxes or pots to allow ready movement, since they generally require a period of 'weaning' before they can exist without constant watering. On larger units this is allowed for by having a section of bench where the mist application is controlled by a time mechanism, called a weaning unit. More generally, however, moving the leaf near the nozzle or moving the boxes or pots to the edge of the mist zone is acceptable. Other methods of weaning are also provided. Preferably there should also be gradual reduction of root temperature. In recent years there has been less emphasis on weaning. Apart from this there is the obvious difficulty of cuttings being at various stages of growth, but one can soon work things out with a little experience.

PLANNING A MIST UNIT
To order a mist unit it is necessary to send details of the bench size and water pressure to the supplier of the equipment, who will then quote for the complete unit — soil warming cables, nozzles, leaf, the associated equipment, and will also provide instructions for setting up their particular equipment.

USING A MIST UNIT
Soft or hard cuttings of many types of plants can be rooted in mist units. Plants with very hairy soft leaves however tend to rot since the moisture lies too long on them. Cuttings can be taken at almost any time of year, because conditions under mist units are ideal for root development. Indeed the mist propagation unit is a godsend to the gardener anxious to increase stocks of all shrubs, trees and house plants. Mist units are also very useful for the germination of seeds. This is especially true with difficult items such as primulas or begonias.

Apart from ensuring a good clean water supply, along with the necessary water pressure, mist units are relatively trouble free. In areas where the water contains a lot of lime, a deposit can be left on the leaves, but this, although you may think it unsightly, is not normally detrimental except perhaps to heathers or rhododendrons.

SPECIAL NOTE — When potting plants which have been rooted in mist, care must be taken to avoid damage to what are very often brittle 'water' roots which snap off very easily.

Mist propagation. The first picture shows the type of mist nozzle used in this propagation. The second picture shows the mist being sprayed out of the nozzle

9 Lighting Your Greenhouse

Two totally different things are embraced in this chapter. One is lighting your greenhouse so you can see your way round it on long winter evenings.

The other is purely for the benefit of the plants.

1. WORKING LIGHT

This is to allow you to work in the evening, especially when you have to get on with things on a winter evening or simply provide better light on a dull day. Here tungsten filament lights (the type used in the home) are involved. The important thing is to position the light or lights to give the best effect. Waterproof light fittings and connections are essential, especially in a metal greenhouse.

2. DAY LENGTH ALTERATION OR NIGHT BREAK

This involves the control of the flowering season of a wide range of plants of which chrysanthemums are perhaps the best known. Low intensity light (with tungsten filament) is usually used to create artificial long days. The loading is 5-10 watts per square foot, which in simple terms means that a 100 watt unit will cover 10-20 square feet.

Basically what happens is that plants such as chrysanthemums which begin to form their buds when the day's light is less than 12-13 hours, are prevented from doing so by making the day artificially longer. Two hours of extra light in August/September, April and May, 3-4 hours in October, November, February and March and 5 hours in December is usual. The extra light is usually given in the middle of the night. Once the lighting period ceases, short days resume and the plants then bud and proceed to flower, which must be done according to progress. Readers are advised to refer to a specialised work on the subject — *The Complete Book of the Greenhouse* — I.G. Walls; *Chrysanthemums the Year Round* — Searle & Machin.

3. SUPPLEMENTARY LIGHT
This is the area where the ambitious gardener can really go to town. It is pretty obvious from the dejected look of many plants in the dull winter days that they are resenting the poor light. This is especially so for many seedlings such as tomatoes in the spring. Two or three 20 watt fluorescent tubes 6 inches apart, suspended above the plants (12-18 inches or so) can work wonders during dull weather. Many plants, including tomatoes, need a period of darkness (7-8 hours), but many bedding plants are capable of responding to continuous light and grow very quickly to prove it.

Other very bright lamps are available, such as Mercury Vapour lamps of special type, which will treat quite a large area of bench. They are generally suspended about 3 feet above the plants being treated.

On no account use ordinary incandescent bulbs to try to help plants grow. These bulbs give off more heat than light, and you need them close enough to the plants to scorch them in order to provide enough light. Stick to fluorescent tubes.

GROWING ROOMS
Here artificial light replaces natural light, generally in solid buildings of high thermal insulation, as distinct from a greenhouse. Cupboards, cellars and other areas are often suitable. Bulbs such as daffodils or tulips can be flowered beautifully in dark cupboards with only tungsten filament lamps suspended about 12 inches above the leaf tips. Often too the heat from the lamps is quite enough to keep the bulbs sufficiently warm without resorting to other means of heat although it is wise to have thermostatically controlled electric heaters available during the dark period. For bulbs 12 hours light in each 24 is given. It should be realised, of course, that with most bulbs the flower is complete within the bulb and it

is only the influence of low intensity light which is required to spark off the vital process of growth.

In the case of plants which require bright light, it is necessary to use banks of fluorescent tubes set up in various ways, to give a level of illumination of between 500 and 1000 lumens (5,000-10,000 lux). While many plants will respond to 24 hours continuous light, others are not capable of doing so.

Important Note The various ways of using artificial light to best advantage are not within the scope of this book. Gardeners anxious for additional information are strongly advised to contact their local Electricity Board, where specialist information can generally be obtained.

It cannot be emphasised too strongly that where electricity and plants are involved, strict safety precautions must be adhered to.

10 Growing Mixes

There are so many readily available composts on the market today that it may seem pointless for the gardener to mix his own. This is especially true when one considers the problem of soil sterilization.

Nevertheless on grounds of cost and for other reasons, many gardeners do wish to make up their own growing mixes, and like all the fun of doing so too. But if you do buy composts, remember to buy them for a particular purpose, e.g. rooting cuttings, sowing seeds, potting on young or mature plants. This is important, although it may not seem to be, since fertilizer levels vary in different mixes.

As regular liquid feeding is carried out in soilless mixes, the actual quantity of fertilizer included is not vital.

PROPAGATING COMPOST
For the rooting of cuttings in mist or generally.
> 50% peat of good brown texture (not black and humic)
> 50% sand (coarser for mist)

To each bushel (22 x 10 x 10 inches) add 4 oz ground limestone (or 1 oz per 2 gallon bucket). *Do not add lime for ericaceous subjects.*

SEED SOWING COMPOST (soilless)
> 75% good brown peat
> 25% sand or gravel

To each bushel add 3-4 oz slow release complete trace element fertilizer (e.g. Vitax Q4, Foremost CF1, Osmocote, according to directions.)

GROWING COMPOSTS

For growing a wide range of plants, using the lesser amount of fertilizer for young plants and the greater amount for mature plants.

Add 5-6 oz ground limestone per bushel ($1\frac{1}{2}$ oz per 2 gallon bucket, and 2-8 oz complete trace element containing fertilizer (2 oz per bucket).

JOHN INNES COMPOST

Seed Compost:

    2 parts sterilized loam, by bulk
    1 part peat by bulk
    1 part sand by bulk

Plus $1\frac{1}{2}$ oz superphosphate of lime and $\frac{3}{4}$ oz ground limestone per bushel.

No. 1 Potting Compost   For growing young plants.

    7 parts sterilized loam, by bulk
    3 parts peat by bulk
    2 parts sand by bulk

Plus 4 oz J.I. Base per bushel and $\frac{3}{4}$ oz chalk.

No. 2 Potting Compost   For general use in the summer, including tomatoes.

    As above + 8 oz J.I. Base and
    $1\frac{1}{2}$ oz chalk per bushel.

No. 3 Potting Compost   For chrysanthemums and large plants.

    As above + 12 oz J.I. Base and
    $2\frac{1}{2}$ oz chalk per bushel

John Innes Base

    2 parts by weight hoof & horn, $\frac{1}{8}$ in grist
    (13 per cent nitrogen)
    2 parts by weight superphosphate (18 per cent
    phosphoric acid)
    1 part by weight sulphate of potash
    (48 per cent to 50 per cent potash)

MIXING COMPOST

The important thing with all composts is to mix clean ingredients on a clean surface and mix them thoroughly. Remember that it is the total bulk of the mixed compost which is used as a basis for the amount of fertilizer. In general this means that you must allow for about one third shrinkage, i.e. 3 bushels becomes 2, 3 buckets — $2\frac{1}{2}$ and so on.

It is essential to turn the compost several times, since if you merely scatter the fertilizer on without adequate turning you will finish up with concentrated patches of fertilizer, which can be injurious to plants. Conversely there could be areas with no fertilizer at all and plants would starve.

BARK COMPOSTS

Of increasing interest these days is the use of pulverized bark which results in a compost very similar in texture to peat. As there tends to be a temporary shortage of the element nitrogen in bark, extra supplies of this should be given to the plants.

HYDROPONICS

Also of increasing interest to gardeners is the use of inert aggregate, where all the plants' nutrient supplies are provided by complete spectrum liquid fertilizers, such as Maxicrop Tomato Special.

There are various forms of hydroponics, including the latest which involves shallow polythene troughs through

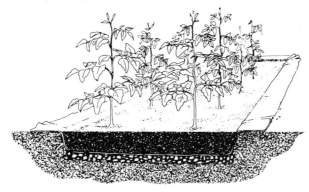

A simple hydroponics system

A simple hydroponics system showing circulating tank

which a fine film of nutrient solution is constantly passed.

The simplest hydroponics system and the easiest to manage, is made by taking out a trench some 3 feet wide and 6-8 inches deep. Put some good rough material in the base of the trench and then line it with polythene. Holes are made in the polythene 2-3 inches from the base. Into the trench is put inert aggregate such as vermiculite, lignite or even coarse sand. A reservoir of moisture remains below the drainage holes and this is pulled up by the plants. Constant feeding and watering with a complete liquid nutrient is essential from the outset. Results can be quite spectacular under this system and the same aggregate can be used again and again if well flushed out with plain water at the end of the crop.

FERTILIZERS — SOLID AND LIQUID

There is a vast range of fertilizers available today, solid for scattering on dry or mixing with compost, others for diluting and applying in water. Manufacturers of all fertilizers give clear directions of:

a) type of fertilizer — solid or liquid, and what crops it can best be used for according to its balance or percentage of nutrient.

b) the exact rate of application or dilution rate — which must be adhered to otherwise plants can be either under or overfed.

c) The frequency of application of the fertilizer or liquid food.

11 Getting Results with Propagators

Plants, like ourselves, sweat. Botanists call it transpiration. It is in a way like breathing, and is a more or less continuous process, dependent on the temperature of the air and, perhaps still more important, the amount of water vapour in the air. A fair indication of the level of humidity in a greenhouse can be obtained by coming into the greenhouse first thing in the morning. It will then frequently be steamed up and the plants often wet and dripping. This is due to the moisture in the air condensing out as the air cools at night. Excess condensation is not too good a thing with plants like tomatoes since it can spoil the fruit, but for propagation and in fact starting off all new plants, whether from seed or cuttings, a high level of humidity is desirable. This is because seed, or more specially a section of plant removed without roots (or even with them) is seldom capable of absorbing or sucking up moisture in sufficient quantity, because if has no effective means of doing so. This is more so when the atmosphere is hot and dry as any moisture the little plant can take up is quickly sweated or transpired into the air. Think of a parched desert and you will get the general idea. This results in the seed and its young shoots drying out, or, in the case of cuttings, wilting or collapsing, as you have seen happen many times. This state of affairs is certainly not helpful to any young plant, especially a cutting seeking to make its own roots and become self dependent. It is for this reason that it is usually helpful to keep the atmosphere moist and muggy to avoid the danger of the plants drying out, since any moisture the plant can take up is not passed immediately into the hot dry atmosphere. Here it helps to think of a steamy jungle and how sticky we would get. A further aspect is the need to induce the seed to germinate in the first case by softening the seed coat so that enough moisture can get into the little plant contained in the seed to trigger off its growth.

AIDS TO PROPAGATION

Propagating Cases   These are by no means new. Pit lights, as they were called, have been used by gardeners for centuries· and feature in nearly all the older gardening books. Here a section of bench was built up high like a frame and the top covered with an extremely heavy and cumbersome wooden frame glazed with glass. Underneath the bench were water filled heating pipes. The result was that inside the frame a warm, muggy atmosphere was provided for rooting cuttings, seed germination and other activities demanding such conditions. Such heavy cumbersome frames have little place in a modern greenhouse and in recent years several things have happened to make propagating cases more manageable.

The first and perhaps most important development is the availability of electrically heated self-contained propagating cases, which in effect are mini-greenhouses. I know they can be expensive, but what a boon they are. All that is necessary is to install them in a light spot on the greenhouse bench. Because of the small total area involved, the cost of heating these cases is negligible, which these days is a major consideration. Their top is so shaped that the water, which inevitably condenses on the underside of the glass runs conveniently to the side instead of dripping on to the plants. Access, ventilation and watering facilities are well provided for.

The more sophisticated propagating cases are complete with thermostat and it is only a question of connecting them up to a suitable electricity supply. They are also available with capillary self watering systems, which means still less work for you.

Self-made Propagating Cases   Any handyman gardener good with tools and bits and pieces can readily make himself a propagating case. It is necessary first to make a small cold frame with either a polythene or Dutch light sash on top to

80

create the hot, muggy atmosphere. Heating is supplied from below with soil warming cables to a loading of 7·5 watts per square foot. The case should be bench mounted (2ft 6 in x 3ft) or bigger if necessary, 12 inches deep at rear and 9 inches at the front to give a slope for moisture run. The sides can be made of wood, or better still, glass, the glass being supported by a light wooden framework.

There should be facilities for supporting the top open slightly for ventilation and fully opening for watering inside the frame. This is especially important when glass is used in the top cover to avoid accidents.

Dome Covers for Plastic Trays   The advent of plastic seed trays and clear plastic dome covers for them has brought a whole new area of possibilities into gardening. Particularly useful and clean is the Jiffy Hobby Garden which contains Jiffy 7's (compressed peat pellets) which expand on wetting. The Jiffy's, 24 in number, fit into indentations in the base of the tray. The light plastic dome cover allows ventilation around the side and furthermore also allows water to enter at the side so that the Jiffy 7's can take up water from below. This is very useful as it avoids disturbing any seeds sown on top of the Jiffy 7's. These Hobby Gardens can of course be used for a wide range of propagating activities.

Ordinary plastic seed trays, with the dome covers available to fit them, can of course be used for seed sowing or rooting of cuttings, as they give an ideal muggy climate. Some have ventilation facilities in the form of a little vent in the top.

A useful item of equipment is a heated base on which to stand the plastic trays. Where, however, a whole bench has soil warming cables installed, the trays are simply placed on the bench for the most efficient use of heat. Indeed it is doubtful whether one could find a better way of raising seeds and rooting cuttings at lower cost and with the minimum of worry and I now use them almost exclusively for everything from seed sowing to rooting dahlias and chrysanths.

Terraria   The use of artificial light has already been discussed, terraria is simply a propagating case with fluorescent tubes which give complete climate control, in-

▲ A modern propagator. The Autogrow P40F designed as a plant propagating unit with soil-warming cables, controlled by a thermostat (*courtesy of Autogrow*)

▼ A fully automatic propagating case (*courtesy of Humex*)

◀ Mini propagators can be placed on heated bases to give a rise of between 5 and 10 degrees to the soil inside the propagator (*courtesy of Humex*)

cluding light intensity, contained in a unit of reasonable size. This means that light demanding plants can be grown even in the dull winter days, instead of becoming drawn and spindly, typical of plants grown in greenhouses in a dull winter. Here again we are talking in terms of quite a bit of money and it is of course possible to rig up lights over a heated bench with excellent results, particularly in areas poor in winter light.

Polythene Bags and Drapes   A very cheap way of making a very simple propagating case providing an ideal container for seed sowing or the taking of cuttings, is by placing a polythene bag over a pot. This bag can be supported with a little stick or wire hoop. The same can be done with boxes and trays, using larger bags.

A newer system which is finding favour for the taking of shrub cuttings, particularly in summer, is to have a high sided bench heated either by pipes underneath or soil warming cables, over which is placed a tent of white or green

Polythene tents suitable for use in propagating plants in the greenhouse

polythene. Much used commercially, this is a system which appears to find favour with most gardeners. The coloured polythene seems to allow the type of light through it which induces quick rooting in a lot of different species. It also seems to have much value for seed germination.

Some hints to help you get the best of Propagators   In the humid atmosphere which prevails in all propagators in closed atmospheres, good drainage of compost is essential. Composts of poor texture will become soggy on the surface, which excludes air and slows rooting. Always use rough sand or gravel in the compost.

Many proprietary, ready-mixed propagating composts or growing mixes are available for sale and the texture of these is usually satisfactory. Always avoid using home-made compost of poor texture or you are certain to get a high rate of failure despite having done everything else right. A further point of importance is **not** to firm composts in trays or pots unduly as this further restricts drainage.

For batches of soft cuttings recently removed from the parent plants a little shade with green polythene or even newspaper can be helpful for a day or so until they begin to pick up, even in the hot air of a propagating case. Put cuttings on an open bench and you will note that they can wilt very badly in sunny weather despite shading, unless of course you have mist propagation.

It should not be necessary to water pots, trays or boxes in propagating cases or under cover so often as when on the open bench.

When water is required use only a fine rose watering can. Alternatively stand the containers in trays of water for a short while.

Drips should be occasionally removed from the inside of the glass of propagating cases, dome covers, or polythene to avoid the compost being washed away from the cuttings or seeds by persistent dripping on one spot.

POTS AND CONTAINERS
The range of pots and containers available today is so bewildering that it is difficult to decide what best to buy.

Clay pots are still available but are now very expensive. They are available in various sizes, a good average size for a range of house plants being about 5-6 inches. Clay pots lose moisture through their sides, which means a lot more watering for you. In addition they quickly get covered with algae and scum, which although not harmful to the plants, is not nice to look at. Clay pots do not work very well on capillary benches either, since although the compost does suck up some moisture, a lot of this is lost before it gets to the top of the pot. Clay pots get broken so easily too.

Plastic pots   are all the vogue now and have many virtues. Apart from cleanliness they go through less water than clay pots and are a lot easier to keep clean.

Polypropylene   pots are also available, it being simplicity itself to wash them in a bucket of warm water. They come in all sorts of shapes and sizes and are still relatively cheap. They are brittle, however, so need a little care.

Seed Trays   Wooden seed boxes are still available, but are being ousted by plastic trays, which come in various depths and sizes. Transparent dome covers are available to fit several sizes of plastic trays, which is very useful for seed sowing and taking cuttings. The tendency these days is to go for shallow trays so that less compost is used and the little seedlings suffer less check when moved, which I suppose is a good enough reason for making them smaller. Many gardeners still prefer to use old fish boxes, which is fair enough if you can still get them. Trays are also available in polypropylene which, although warm, are brittle.

Paper pots   Various types of paper pots can be bought, the most popular of which is the whalehide pot which is really just bituminised paper or cardboard. They are very handy for growing on tomatoes, cucumbers, lettuce or other plants intended for planting out. The paper pots can be left on, but preferably should be torn off if no root damage ensues. In any case by the time plants are ready for planting out the paper is usually rotted. The strongest types of whalehide pots are used for tomatoes in ring or peat mattress culture, the size here being the 9 inch pot with or without a base, according to whether you are planting the tomatoes in position or not.

Peat Pots and Trays   A range of peat pots, either round or square, are available. Peat trays can also be bought. Peat pots have the great advantage of allowing the roots of the plant to come through the peat, so that the whole thing is popped into a larger pot or the ground, completely avoiding any planting check. This is true with all peat pots and trays of any size. The only trouble you are likely to get is a temporary shortage of the element nitrogen, which arises during the decomposition process of the peat/wad material from which the pot is made. This can be overcome by giving a little extra feeding.

Soil and Peat Blocks   These were popular in the 50's and are once more getting more popular, especially peat blocks, made with special block makers from a wet peat sog.

Plastic blocks as containers are now also available. The smaller size blocks are used only for young plants for a limited time.

Jiffy 7's & Peat Pellets   These are made of compressed peat in a netting material which expand on wetting. They contain sufficient quantities of plant nutrients for a limited period and are excellent for seed sowing, striking cuttings or pricking off young plants.

Other Receptacles   A wide range of items can now be bought for growing plants, including polythene pots, bolsters (which are polythene bags full of peat compost with sections of the top removed and ideal for tomatoes) and receptacles of mineral wool and other materials.

All have their virtues for varying systems of culture and different plants.

12 Plants and Temperature Ranges

Despite what has been said about the temperature requirements of plants, it is worth bearing in mind that many plants would tolerate a wide range of temperatures. There is no need to waste heat when they can be grown satisfactorily at lower temperatures. Many plants will grow happily at lower temperatures than those considered ideal. These days no one can afford to waste heat at the cost it is and we do not have solar heat units for greenhouses yet. But do bear in mind that some regions of the country are warmer than others, and this can make a lot of difference.

Having said this, many plants can be grown in the spring and summer months with no artificial heat at all, relying entirely on the sun.

Here are some of the most popular plants and the temperature ranges they will succeed in.

VEGETABLES

Lettuce are hardy and can be grown more or less completely cold in any part of the country, provided you pick the right variety. With a little frost protection, however, they can grow a lot quicker in winter. They are a lot more tender to eat too. Poor light and dampness in winter tends to slow up production very considerably, especially in the north and in poor light areas, and you could be a little disappointed with results in those areas. But from February until May or even June conditions are excellent in the cool greenhouse and you can grow really succulent lettuce to please any palate, however fastidious. The same is true from September till November or December in reasonable light areas.

Tomatoes can be grown completely cold from May to September but are much more productive with a longer season of growth. Provided you can maintain a minimum night temperature of around 13°C tomatoes can be planted as early as February. This will cost you a lot of fuel no matter what heating system you have, unless you have the home central heating boiler in the greenhouse. Planting in late March is possible in the reasonably well heated greenhouse, mid-April for the mildly heated greenhouse and of course May for cold tomatoes (April in mild, early areas). Some heat, especially at night, is beneficial in most areas, especially during April and May, and again during September and October, to avoid overnight dampness and to keep the fruit nice and tender.

Cucumbers These need much the same treatment as tomatoes. They can be grown cold from May until September and are specially suitable for bench culture after early seed sowing and rooting of cuttings is over for the season. They make a pleasant addition to any salad.

Melons These like heat and warmth but can be grown as a short-term cold crop from May till September, and really tasty they are too and very simple to grow. With heat they can be planted in April.

Other vegetables which can be grown in greenhouses with little heat are sweet peppers, vegetable marrows, French beans, and many more. The whole range of outdoor vegetables such as carrots, beetroot, onions, peas, turnips and so on can be produced a lot earlier under glass than out of doors, provided you have space in the greenhouse borders. More usually the early crops are grown in frames or cloches out of doors, simply because the greenhouse is needed for other things. In addition a wide range of vegetables such as cabbage, cauliflower, and many more can be sown in the greenhouse for planting out of doors later.

FRUIT

Vines can be grown either in warm or cool conditions, but take up a lot of room and in a small greenhouse you really are not going to get a sufficient quantity of grapes to eat or make a lot of wine. They will crop earlier with heat, but cold vine growing can be very rewarding.

Peaches and Nectarines are also excellent for cool greenhouses but are again greedy on space. Nevertheless they are very succulent.

Figs are an interesting subject for the odd corner and will grow and fruit according to the temperature level available. They need vigorous restriction in a small greenhouse.

Strawberries can be grown beautifully and are really tasty in a cool or heated greenhouse but are not always conveniently handled. It is best to pot up runners in 6 inch pots in July and bring under cover in December/January. Without heat they can produce succulent fruit during May, when they are very expensive in the shops.

Most fruits — apples, pears, and so on can be grown in pots to perfection in a cool greenhouse, buying special pot grown trees and putting them in large pots in the autumn, the pots being left outside until early spring when growth is starting.

BEDDING PLANTS

A wide range of bedding plants can be grown under relatively cool conditions and you can really save a lot of money here by raising your own. For good germination of seed in February/March warmth is needed. The localised heat of a soil warmed bench or propagating case is ideal. Much can be done by sowing seed in plastic trays with dome covers in the home. Thereafter plants can be grown in temperatures which do not fall much below 10°C at night. Bedding plants are usually put into cold frames by April.

FLOWER CROPS OUT OF DOORS

Dahlias and chrysanthemums are examples of plants which

90

can be readily started in a frost-free greenhouse (chrysanthemums can, of course, survive frost) for subsequent planting out of doors to give an early show of bloom. For early rooting of cuttings the localised warmth of a propagating case or soil warmed bench is really necessary for best results. Again much can also be done in the home.

POT PLANTS
As with bedding plants, warmth is preferable for seed sowing or rooting cuttings before May. This can readily be achieved in a propagating case. Items such as primulas, impatiens, pelargoniums (geraniums) and many more can be grown early in a completely cold greenhouse. Earlier propagation with some warmth is desirable to give a longer season of colour, however.

CHRYSANTHEMUMS (indoor)
Chrysanthemums can be grown as an indoor crop completely cold from April to September and how valuable they are in the autumn for cut bloom. More usually, as discussed above, they are propagated in a greenhouse in March/April in warmth, grown out of doors during the summer months, and brought into frost-free (7°C) conditions in September.

BULBS
A wide range of bulbs can be grown to sheer perfection either in mild heat or cold in the greenhouse. These include tulips, hyacinths, daffodils, gladioli, and many more. Warmth will merely influence the time of flowering and most of the better known bulbs are hardy in any case.

CACTI
A wide range of cacti can be grown in relatively cool conditions, but few, if any, will withstand frost, which means keeping them frost free.

ORCHIDS
Exotic types need heat, but several can be grown cool.

ALPINES AND SHRUBS

As most alpine or rock plants and shrubs are hardy, growing them under glass merely gives an earlier and in many cases a more sustained and prolific period of flowering. Do remember to give them a good quality compost and a covering of gravel on top of the pot too.

Index

0
INCH CM
1
2
1
3
4
2 5
6
7
3
8
9
4 10
11
5 12
13
14
15
6
16
17
7
18